Incomprehensible Lesson

Poems by FAWZI KARIM
in versions by ANTHONY HOWELL
after translations made by the author

BORN IN BAGHDAD in 1945 and now living in London, Fawzi Karim is rapidly establishing a reputation as a major figure in contemporary poetry. *Plague Lands*, his first book of poems in translation, was a Poetry Book Society recommendation for 2011.

ANTHONY HOWELL's first collection *Inside the Castle* was brought out in 1969. His most recent book of poems is *From Inside*, The High Window Press, 2017.

T0095960

Incomprehensible Lesson

Fawzi Karim

in versions by

Anthony Howell

CARCANET

ACKNOWLEDGEMENTS

The poems included here in 'The Empty Quarter' first appeared in a chapbook of that title published by Grey Suit Editions, 2014. 'Usual Story', 'The Painting', 'The Night drives in its Nails' and 'The Balloon' all appeared in *Modern Poetry in Translation*. 'Patrolman' and 'Over Hastily' appeared in *The Next Review*. 'Central Line' was published in *Ambit*.

First published in Great Britain in 2019 by
Carcanet
Alliance House, 30 Cross Street
Manchester M2 7AQ
www.carcanet.co.uk

Text copyright © Fawzi Karim & Anthony Howell 2019

The right of Fawzi Karim and Anthony Howell to be identified as the authors of this work has been asserted in accordance with the Copyright, Designs and Patents Act of 1988; all rights reserved.

A CIP catalogue record for this book is
available from the British Library,
ISBN 978 1 78410 428 3

Book design by Andrew Latimer
Printed in Great Britain by SRP Ltd, Exeter, Devon

The publisher acknowledges financial
assistance from Arts Council England.

Contents

Incomprehensible Lesson

Introduction

In the poem 'The Empty Quarter', I tried to confront the time of my exile in London, while I tried before that to regain the experience of a homeland in my earlier poem 'Plague Lands'.

My sense of my own homeland faded with Baghdad, which has itself gradually faded during the war years, since the early eighties until now. My sense of it has faded with the demise of my neighbourhood 'al Abbassiyya', faded with my boat in the Tigris river, and with the palm trees next to the house; faded with the berries and oleander inside the house, with the house itself. I felt all this when I returned to Baghdad, after the 2003 war, and after the end of the dictatorship. It dawned on me vividly that my time there had completely faded, leaving hardly a mark. 'Plague Lands' was an attempt to restore it, through memory fused with the imagination. Thus my memory was expanded, enhanced, in order to transcend time, to transcend history and enter myth, enter the domain of poetry.

The time of my exile in London, in the poem 'Empty Quarter', moves at a different pace to my circulation. I tried, since I came to this great city in early 1979, to adapt to the fast pace of life here, but it feels like a very fast pace, which does not respond to the slow pace of my inner time, poetic time, the time of the Eastern cafe, in which I feel that I swim, in the slow current of the Tigris, without having to look at my wristwatch, or waiting for something to happen. There is a hint in the 'Empty Quarter', that may easily be missed, about the threshold – where 'Tigris Time' crosses over into the time of exile:

> Why would the passers-by
>> bother to notice
>> a tramp out of time with all tourists?
> He stands there, gaunt as a telephone pole,
>> hoping, but for what?
> No one sees the huge locked door that looms there,
>> right in front of him;
> A weathered door that stops him
>> from breaking into the hubbub of London.
> First reaction? Back into the head.
> Time is not counted in seconds here,
>> but in the ripples as they pass.

The desire to vanish, which is present in all my poems, is an expression of the desire to belong to this internal time, this poetic time. To transform history into myth, the time of memory into the time of the imagination, is to transcend the time of hours and days, and enter the myth that exists without time. I think that this transcendence is the most important fruit of the tree of exile, which thus took on a metaphysical dimension.

Traditional Arabic poetry did not help me much in this, with the exception of the unusual voices of Abu Nuwas, and al-Ma'arri, because Arab poetry is generally either restricted to the five senses, and driven by sensual obsession, or taken up with generalised abstract ideas. The poem in which passion might ascend to the plane of thought has remained in the shadows. An older Eastern poetry (Persian, Indian, Chinese), rather than Arabic poetry, has become a haven for me. Sensory dominance and abstract ideas inform our modern Arab poetry as well as the tradition. All too often, the poet relies on great ideas: political, social, religious or ideological. Even modernity, where an Arab voice may simulate the literature of the West, has became a doctrine, spoiled by a touch of sanctity. Therefore our modern poet is characterized as a prophet with a bloated ego and a sense of certainty. You can see such a tendency in al Mutanabbi in the past, and in Adonis in our time. This brand of poet knows, when he writes his poem, what he wants before he begins the first line, because he writes his poem under a banner, informed by some great idea. The most prominent poets of our time are poets of the banner, poets of conviction. The poem that enters the maze with its first line is rare.

The poets of the maze are few, and they live in the shadows, in the way that al Ma'arri used to live in the past, or as al Sayyab, al Brekan and Abdul Saboor exist in the present.

Use of the verbal magic in the Arabic language is an instinctive trait among Arab poets since the pre-Islamic period, and has only been strengthened by the 'Koran', which made Arabic a sacred language. Ancient and modern poets have trod carefully and even perhaps too cautiously in also allowing poetry to be thought-provoking, and capable of taking its readers well beyond the surface of the word, beyond the power in its sound, and beyond the sheer eloquence of the sentence. In the past, our poets demonstrated an enthusiasm for al Jahiz (the great critic of the eighth century) when he expressed his preference for the form/shape/sound of the word to its meaning, and they get excited today with regard to a deconstructive criticism that analyses the signifier at the cost of the signified.

Taking their cue from al Jahiz, a lot of Arab poets and critics have become enchanted by the modernist denial of content, which they found abundant in contemporary

French poetry and criticism. The spark of this abstract tendency began in Morocco and Beirut, where the French language was really the prevailing language among intellectuals of literature. It then widened its influence to cover the best part of the Arab world, so books which even had titles that could not be understood became best-sellers.

English, in comparison, had less impact on the poetry and criticism of the sixties generation, and that neglect of English poetry persists to this day.

To despotic regimes in the Arab world, this absence of meaning has been a gift – engendering a silence about matters that they never imagined could be achieved at such a low cost.

2

A poem called 'Song of Rain' by al Sayyab has the following line:

Do you know what sort of grief the rain sends?

Critics observed that al Sayyab was influenced here by Edith Sitwell, and regretted this, because the rain in our climate is a testament to goodness. How then can it arouse grief to the heart of the poet!

Our critics invariably approach the poem via theory. They do not realize that the feelings of the poet here come from a source which is a mystery. I can have such feelings towards the rain (perhaps because I live in Greenford!) – and towards the sadness of its falling which also has a natural and divine beauty… I call it the metaphysical dimension of poetry.

I think that this metaphysical dimension is fundamental.

In western poetry, part of the reaction against the romantic strain, is to deny any significant relationship between poetry and mystery. Archibald McLeish has a phrase: 'A poem should not mean but be,' which expresses the desire of a number of poets, to be thought of as skilled makers creating an artefact, rather than perceived as Seers. I prefer to be a Seer.

I would like to mention here that some of the theories of intellectuals in the West about poetry and its criticism cannot escape being considered as corrupted by the phenomenon of a society revelling in its prosperity. There is a dearth of adventurous ideas, and in their place a reliance on techniques and displays associated with the field of pure form.

'Freedom of choice is being misused today by Western writers', writes the Polish poet Czesław Milosz, 'for the purpose of creating dehumanized literature perhaps, it is true, under the pretext of rebelling against a dehumanized world. But are the western writers themselves conscious of the difference between genuine concern and what is just subservience to fashion or a marketing device?'

When encountering the wave of East European poetry translated into the languages of the capitalist West in the fifties and after, English poets were enthusiastic about this fresh humanitarian voice in poetry – coming from the heart of suffering, from the heart of life. The desire to take advantage of this has changed a lot of their abstract tendencies.

Recent Arab poets and critics of poetry (with access, as I see it, to a poetic voice that comes from the heart of suffering) nevertheless deceive themselves on a permanent basis: they seem willing to mimic poets and critics in the West in their 'subservience to fashion or to a marketing device'. They neglect to take note of the poets in Eastern

Europe, who have suffered, like them, from the scourge of totalitarianism, and from the worship of some 'great idea' at the expense of a more humane expression. They are afraid that if they looked towards these poets of eastern Europe, they might see themselves in the mirror, and this would bring home to them that they remain outside of western modernity.

The poet and his critic in our Arabic literature today will avoid this mirror at all costs. The Arab poet may well prefer a self-deception dictated by an illusory feeling of being on a par with western poets and critics.

3

In the sixties, the publication of books of poetry, especially in Beirut, reached a very high level. Readers became accustomed to following the news of poetry and poets through a number of literary and poetic magazines such as 'al Adab', 'al Adeeb', 'Shir' magazine and 'Mawaqif' - as well as through the poetic publications brought out by the major publishing houses. We were familiar with the poets who came before us - al Sayyab, al-Bayati, Baland al Haidari, Nazik al Malaike, Adonis, Salah Abdul Saboor, Khalil Hawi, Nizar Qabbani, Yusuf al-Khal, Hijazi, Saadi Youssef - and we used to follow their poems through their books. Readers relied on a book of poetry when assessing the worth of a poet.

However, in Iraq, when the Baath Party came to power, this totalitarian regime instigated the phenomenon of 'the festival of poetry', and their cultural media ensured that this became well known and influential. Other Arab regimes saw the benefit of this and quickly followed the Baathist example. The official media channels were quick to direct such performing poets to the ethos of the targets it had an interest in implementing. The media also started to highlight the phenomenon of the 'star' poet. Thus, the published book of poetry was gradually put into the shade, and after that consigned to darkness. All the publishing houses, those in Beirut, as well as in the other capitals of the Arab world, have now come to rely financially on the official institutions of their governments.

The 'sixties' generation in Iraq was leftist for the most part, and often Marxist, and they were subjected to a great deal of intimidation. The dominance of the cultural festival has consigned most of these poets to obscurity, and many of them have had to flee Iraq.

A book of poetry is no longer the standard in the evaluation of a poet. The festivals of poetry and access to the cultural media are what confer esteem to the poet, and put him or her under the spotlight, as far as the public at large are concerned. The survival of a handful of the Iraqi poets from the sixties today is the product of their own courageous resistance to oblivion.

4

I came to London on the run from a nightmare. My nation and the Arab world has brought me more than enough suffering, and it is this that makes me sense my responsibility so intensely. It obliges me to put humanity in the foreground, rather than an idea.

London finally brought with it the opportunity to read English, and this raised a window on the poetry of the whole world. So vast did this ocean of poetry appear that I sensed myself shrinking, until I became no more than the atom of Lucretius. But London in its generosity has also given me the wonder of classical music. This in its turn has raised a window on the universe and beyond, until I sense that I am able to hear the Pythagorean music of the planets.

Poetry is the twin brother of music. And to this day, when I write a poem on the keyboard of my computer, I experience a liberation from the limitations of language and its restrictions, and enjoy imagining that I am striking the keys of a piano. Each poem I write is accompanied by a melody in my head, making it easier to be rendered loud and clear – as if a song.

5

The poem is written from an ethical obsession not a political one. It belongs to myth, not history. The poem sings, but it is thought also.

Fawzi Karim
London, 2019

*

POETS MENTIONED

Abu Nuwas, great Iraqi poet, (762–813).

Abu al-Ala al-Maarri, great Syrian poet, (973–1057).

Abu at-Tayyib al Mutanabbi, great Iraqi poet, (915–965).

Adonis, Modern Syrian poet, (1930–).

Badir Shakir al-Sayyab, modem Iraqi poet, (1926–1964).

Mahmood al-Brekan, modem Iraqi poet, (1929–2012).

Salah Abd al-Saboor, modem Egyptian poet, (1931–1981).

Abdul Wahab al-Bayati, modem Iraqi poet, (1926–1999).

Buland al-Haidari, modern Iraqi poet, (1926–1996).

Nazik al-Malaike, modern Iraqi poet, (1923–2007).

Khalil Hawi, modern Lebanese, (1919–1982). Nizar Qabbani, modern Syrian poet, (1923–1998).

Yusuf al-Khal, modern Lebanese poet, (1917–1987).

I

In the Shadow of Gilgamesh

In the Shadow of Gilgamesh

Aiming for the sandbanks,
    we float across the Tigris in skiffs of wood and tin.
We set up bivouacs of mats,
    plant beans and cucumbers,
    and from the bowels of the sandy silt
    witness the emergence of a man.
Solid enough, he sports a shield
    made from shipwrecked bones
    and the leads of fishing nets.
Shards of the moon on waves are mirrors in his cloak,
And the fish rise now
    as if they were the echo of his call.
A man who sucks the nectar of our youth,
    as indiscriminate as any honey bee.
Like a wave he overwhelms us all,
    and we are pulled back with the froth.

At night a fire encloses the fish
Grilling in its basket like
    a saint ablaze in his halo.
The flames here catch the sheen
    of the wet desires the sand secretes,
And show how we may parley with a god
    squatting there amid the algae
    covering the bottom of the Tigris.
And now the tavern road appears
    as if the wake of a golden robe
    that leaves a sparkling trail behind
The steps of a whore who visits
    in the middle of some night.

Has sex with the sexiest,
      (fucks the firmest – both in cock and brawn.)

Secretly, just as she comes to us,
      She'll slip away before the dawn;
Gone as clandestinely as she came.

The poet with us knows how to fill his chest
      in order now to tune the strings
And capture Ishtar in his poems' mesh,
      trawling for her in the depths.
And with the rust off ancient words
      from smoke-exhausted lungs,
He feeds a wound, to suffer all the more,
And manages to camouflage our future
      with the paint of legend,
Now when he sings the dawn light shines on his strings,
      and the tick of the hours gets stilled.
The poet sings of Gilgamesh:

'The shepherd who licks the wounds of his flock,
Who violates the virginity of Uruk's maidens.
Who cloaks the shadow of the highest wall with his own.
Who indeed would be bold enough,
      under the sun, to tame such a one but she,
Ishtar, the lady of lip taste, when lip thirsts for lip?
And yet she is the lady of lament,
      shepherdess of corpses – in the line of fire,
      in any war, fought always for good reason.

In a war, there's this dream in our eyes
      that absolves us
      from acknowledging our victims
And it's this cup of wine

that scours the bad luck from our palms.
With that fine fish we made excellent progress to Uruk,
With this barbed wire we slunk off into exile.

'In Ishtar's temple
Shamhat turns the pages of her charms for visitors:
Go on, you temple whore,
Strip those breasts of your hair's allure,
Flirt the naked hillock
      behind a cup of wine, and go down now
      towards the land of wild beasts.
There you will meet with Enkidu.
We kneaded him from clay bonded with our light.
So Shamhat, the taste of his mouth, a honey made of dates,
      is as the taste of your mouth is to him,
His response will have the grip
      of a thousand knotted fibres.

Shamhat hennaed her hair
      and re-applied her lips with pomegranate peels.
She offered forth her breasts
So that they soared free of their captivity.
Their tips touched savage Enkidu,
      and Enkidu soared free as well.

She copied the shape of the cup
From the shape of the place
Where the thighs meet
And she gave him to drink,
      and he enjoyed letting her sip in return
Until he buckled and his head slumped down.
She sipped the grace of the Maker from his blood,
      leaving no trace,
And at this the gazelles

who had seen him as one of themselves
Suddenly scattered before him.

Enkidu knew that a cord had been cut
Severing words
      from the things out of which they were born:

The string — as apart from the song that surpassed it.'

2.
Our two bodies collided.
There was disarray.
We clashed, and went berserk.
Our sweat made a mush of the ground —
As when a wave covers a sandbank
      and the sandbank seems to sigh.
Founders of the illusory city,
We who had laid its corner-stone
      and walled it,
Then usurped its pride
      and scattered all beyond retrieval's reach.

Promptly enough the pennants of war lay trampled,
Stained and soiled
      by blood and mud;
Though these days, from the clotheslines,
      can't you smell the bleach?

I say, Count yourself blessed:
You're like my brother, in that we both
      began in some womb of aloneness.
Blessed that we shared that cup
      on the bank of the Tigris.

Didn't you ensnare me,
Capable hunter, and lead me
To the mirror of your death? Blessed
By love, do tell me now
Why you just won't answer me?
The sadness of that poetry
         that marked your face with its claws,
You know how it enchanted me!
I was trapped in a thicket,
         that sprouted there, between your lips.
Rim of a cup covered by moss,
Hands of corroded copper…
Rust has covered everything.
All we were is yellowed now,
         powdered by the turmeric of death.

You had been created
         just as you would have wished to be,
You triumphed without killing,
         winning the girls without rape:
But God took umbrage, stripped you
         of all your good intentions,
And therefore you withdraw into yourself,
         taking up some corner of *The Gardenia*,
Bent on overcoming the spirit.
So the strength of your handshake ebbs away.

Yearning weeps in your body.

3.
'Two boats, bound together, will not sink,'
        you told me.
'Ah, but a single puncture
        is sure to scuttle the dinghy!'
        I replied.
And now you find yourself drowning!

Death comes to anyone alone,
        offers an end that can hardly be denied,
As a friend reveals his secret to a friend.
Death dines alone,
        like a wolf with a prodigal lamb,
Or water's strength overwhelms the drowning man.

But she came out from behind her wall.
She had her eyes on you,
That lady with the blue shawl,
And she was it, you knew,
        but could she reassure you?
The grate empty in the winter's pang,
The door flimsy in the face of the wind,
The nail in the boot nip-nipping with its fang.

You bent beneath the swirl of that blue shawl,
Just as they may genuflect
        in their holy niche of prayer,
And to see your sad young face
        divided in the mirrors behind your own locked door,
Reiterates the face of the wounded
        stumbling through fields of corpses,
Recalls the look of a fugitive seeking out exile,
The shock of the poet detained
        (a silencer putting its bead through the temple).

A bandsman leans on his instrument,
    in the nightclub's dark, deserted hall.
It's that expression one observes queuing up for an exit visa.
Secretly bleeding at the policed border,
Know they have cut out his tongue,
    so how can he lick his wounds now?

You manage to leave,
While I'm staying on to lament you.

4.
I have dwelt since I was born in my death unknowingly!
My writing has followed my footprints,
All the way through this banished life I've lived.
And yet I have learnt that I was, in my heedless way,
Marking the footsteps of others.

The sandbanks that we sought
    are no more the pride of the Tigris,
And the poet's loot, brought back
    from imagination's journey,
Resembles that promise of an end,
    grinding in its monotony,
That Shahrazad would interrupt at dawn
For Shahriyar, the impatient one,
    in *The Thousand Nights and a Night*.
Losing all hope has taught me
    to substitute Death for hope,
Accepting him as my hirsute pal:
The goalie of those restless strikes into my own goal.

When I wake up, I sip his wine.
He drains my cup when I can't,
    while I doze off to the side.
I dwell in those footsteps of mine,
And the weight of my hope has the weight of straw.

And now their end is so near,
    I will never return in joy to that lost water-hole,
Sump of putrid dregs today,
While in the past it was the place
    where I guess my roots went down…
Now uprooted.

2006

NOTES

Uruk: the city sacred to the Goddess Ishtar – 'town of the sacred
    courtesans'.
The Gardenia: a well-known café and meeting place of intellectuals in
    Baghdad.

10

The Empty Quarter

'No man can live this life and emerge unchanged. He will carry, however faint, the imprint of the desert, the brand which marks the nomad; and he will have within him the yearning to return, weak or insistent according to his nature. For this cruel land can cast a spell which no temperate clime can match.'

WILFRED THESIGER

On the Highest Peak

On the highest peak,
The deer edge towards my retreat,
Soliciting a blessing
From the cradle of my newborn pain.

The deer kneel then turn away.
The eagle will not risk a restless wind.
Empty are the clouds that frequent my retreat,
Presenting fronts darkened by anxiety.

Passing through the clouds I peer down on the city.
Its roofs are stacked with the nests of storks
While its palms are fans for its siesta,
Lending it shade and a breeze for the streets.

There are boats unmoored on its timeless rivers,
But ages of sand drift across well-known features,
And now it's clear that the city looks more like a corpse
Hovered over by wings which end in claws.

Ice forms on my coat and freezes me to my seat.

Paradise of Fools

'Travelling is a fool's paradise. Our first journeys discover to us the indifference of places. At home I dream that at Naples, at Rome, I can be intoxicated with beauty, and lose my sadness. I pack my trunk, embrace my friends, embark on the sea, and at last wake up in Naples, and there beside me is the stern fact, the sad self, unrelenting, identical, that I fled from. I seek the Vatican, and the palaces. I affect to be intoxicated with sights and suggestions, but I am not intoxicated. My giant goes with me wherever I go.'

RALPH WALDO EMERSON

There's little point in wading against
The current of these tiresome days,
Keen to re-negotiate the swamp of our estrangement.

Little reason for the tide to be concerned
About the bones of drowning men,
Or for the sun to rise yet again on a ruin.

It makes no sense for prisoners of war
To barricade their dreams,
And though one returns from a battle-field

One knows it is only a matter of time.
And so, I do not dispute
That roaming is a fools' paradise,

That 'home' is a catwalk between abysses,
And he who puts out to sea
Seeking another shore may lose the coast.

Waiting for the End

Moment of waiting for the end:
Shadow, you share a dangerous game
Here in my bed, be bold now.
Siphon off all that you can from the head,
Steal the web woven by the dream
And utilise the probe of imagination's insect.

Take from the heart the shed skins of its loves,
And don't neglect to glean from slips of the tongue
What every letter sent has sought to mask.
I am in your hands, for until I can be rid
Of the saddle's weight, the bit and the tug of the rein,
I have nothing to go on but hoof-prints,

Like thoughts that sully the still of the night.

Lowfield Road Quartet

I.
And now in al Andalus Square,
As the bird preens, does the light of dawn
Quench this thirst or not?
The dancers turn heavily as millstones
In the orbit of their fear, fear of waking.
The glass turns, the head turns,
    and the waiter hovers, attentive:
'Another shot of araq?'
A woman slips a foot between my feet:
'You want to dance?'
I change into a ball of eagerness in her hands.
She bounces this on the ground and it never comes to rest.
There are loudspeakers fixed to the wall,
And banners where the fates proclaim their warnings.
There's no respite for the dancer,
No respite anywhere but in his fear, fear of waking.
The glass turns and the head turns,
And over me the trees bend.
I keep the withered secrets of their leaves to myself…
And this taut string:
'When will you get back to me?'
'I will be waiting at whatever gate
    your exile cares to choose.

And I will seduce you, or loneliness will make a man of you,
Or panic may take over
    for a while, but don't, don't give up hope…'

A curtain falls between me and my vision of home.

2.
These mirrors turn the horses again
Towards a too bright sun, while the horizon
    arcs across the portholes.
I see strange cities – on so many first time visits!
Each paradise is set before me while Satan whispers
    but actually my caravan crosses a desert of salt.
Blood on the reins, and such a crushing silence!
What do I really see?
There is a wind that makes no sound
    and therefore leaves no echo.
But what a strength there is to this wind!
I can't raise my hand against it, even to adjust my robe.

'Just take my hand and hold on!'
    said Sammer, my son.
I found no corporeal substance behind those hands of his;
Just the dawn, the dew,
    the Jasmine's shivering branches
and there is the youngster, beckoning
'Father, take off your clothes!
    Be naked. Enter the current with me.'
'Not a chance!' I say.

3.
Damp fringes to the carpet that reaches the horizon
    and Sammer is a water-bird and sports a sandy form.
I watch how the windows overflow with fishes flying,
    butterflies extravagant as the feast of Nowruz.
Sammer seems worried about me, 'Come on, come back in!'
    Re-explore the floating bush.
And the wife remonstrates: 'Please, put your dreams away,
    and come, dear, to my balmy bed.
You never endeavour to turn a blind eye
    to anything ever sighed for.
I worry that my butterflies may get mixed with yours,
    my love with your memories.'
But light is all that ever nets that long remembered butterfly.

Ablaze between the ruins of old days,
    it brings me back to the brothel
To crane over screens and peek at Ishtar
    doing a strip in the draught of a ceiling fan.
A dead bird gets chucked out at the audience.

'Come on! Leave your dreams alone
    and enter my warm bed.'
But I remained foolishly dressed
    And wearing that mask of contemplation
Which let my irresponsible mouth
    go flapping on like a jacket folded over an arm.
And so I surrendered to the bird of my time,
Aiming my days at what exactly?
Well..about that they could never be sure.
And as his doubts may strip the poet of clothes
    and throw him naked into the den of his secrets,
So the tempest strips the willow and the lime
    in Lowfield Road.

Among these flying leaves,
I see my elderly neighbour collecting dew from the grass
    in her old straw hat,
And she helps her knees by supporting herself with a hand
As a wing flutters and then disappears.
The snow will come, and I will see your footsteps
In my back garden and will follow them
    as shadows fill the empty prints of shoes.
Washing, plastic flowers, beads and strips in the mud…
    while snow overwhelms the house of my elderly neighbour…

Pain

At dawn, when disturbed by the tramp of their boots,
The full-throated bellow of their songs
        and the swing of their marching arms…

When with due caution, I curl within myself,
Prickly as some hedgehog…
When the dark of a very long night
        gets smeared like mud on the windows…

When the forefinger of the impossible
Starts to pester me from behind the curtains,
When it strokes me, rubs me out,
        scatters my ashes all over the bed…

That's when I won't look back at my memories,
Fearful they will change to salt.
More and more abscesses form on my flesh
        but I can't ask for help…

At dawn, when disturbed by the tramp of their boots…

Heading for the Sea

I have prepared my boat, fish-hook and bait,
Taking with me the cloak of the night
      with its slow stars.
I steal out, torch in hand,
To the sloping bank of the river.
I am alone.
My father also went out alone in his boat.
Will I get any closer to him now,
      before he reaches the open sea?
Will I come alongside him, and under his sail?

I see the silence floating
      with a fine lightness, cork-like.
The lamps are too weak to soften the darkness.

And we used to say: 'The palm shade for us
      after our loads are removed.'

On the river's bank, there's a death-squad
      – ten strong, ten they have killed –
And someone is weeping there.
I know the water only
      by the reflection of each star.
I hope to reach the sea as did my father,
      to scatter proof of how we were.

And we used to sing: 'The sweet ripe dates for us
  and a well-earned rest in the shade.'

On the river bank some armed and naked men
Fill wretched men who cower there with fear.
– There they are! There!
The sound of an explosion.
Then dust in a gust - it covers them.

I recall that scene, and the fugitives
  under glass, as if in a sepia print –
Eyes quick to follow what alerted them:
Time marching blindly with swift steps
  reaping his human crops.

Imagine me without a mouth,
  without even a lung.
Useless as a witness.
Rowing away into darkness
  towards the open sea.

The God of Solitude

Who will go through
The poetry I write about you,
Sort the grain of sand from the speck of gold,
Unafraid of being accused,
If he jotted down his certitude?
No sooner does love smile on a relationship,
Than hatred leers at it too.

Whose is the mask,
And the face behind that mask,
At this hypocritical party?

Who is it behind the curtain
With those unreadable eyes
And the smile one can only call feline?
He neither censors nor urges caution;
And yet he has lost his aura,
Given over his eternal way
And taken up a path of blind coincidence.

If I am a poet of an age
Free from the ferocity of destiny,
I'll not be doomed if I choose to exchange
        this tedious masquerade
For the reed-beds and their fields.

Out there at last, I won't bemoan
The absence of the flute,
There where the God of Solitude
Handles the clay in silence,
Re-enacting Genesis,
Knowing I am watching Him.

Because It Happens Every Day

Because it happens every day
Without announcing its time,

Happens suddenly, just as a comet
Flashes on the night's wrinkled skin,

Or leaves our very moments under threat
Of collapse beneath the weight of our past,

Because it comes and goes,
Because it startles us

With its sudden drop in pressure,
The paper sweats as we start writing.

A sticky tongue
Has left our underwear damp.

We are not its victims but
Its evidence.

Central Line

Close to my home in Greenford,
The carriages roll to a halt. After long moments
They go on to bisect London.

The line takes me (questions harass) 'Where?'
To streets, buildings, parks marred by repetition,
So that I prefer my own blurred reflection.

Then I return by the same red line,
Musing how, from Waterloo Bridge,
The scene's perfection amazed me:

Seemed an artistic print, framed in an exhibition,
How the tourists milling there
Scattered such colours – like a wedding breakfast –

Was it some performance on TV?
A lady at a party broke through my precautions.
I found myself once more in the role of exile.

The line goes on and on. The years
Sit across from me. I take out my passport.
They want to share its pages.

Faust in Casablanca

A typically Arabic night
Peopled by ordeals in the form of ragged clothes,
Yellow phlegm that's spluttered out by street lamps over
    asphalt.
I descend, through the tunnel of the Hotel de Paris,
And out of its darkness, emerge…onto Casablanca
To mess with a restless wave that keeps on catching me.

'If you were as young as me, man,
You could share my togs,
Stick out a foot to tackle mine,
Feint and dodge,
And run your rings around me.'

2.
What's left me of such joys but outspread wings
            that bear me easily, bear me away…?
This Arabic eagle spending his summer
            making up for a winter of lost time
Remains all folded into himself,
Sees a lowland sunrise without sun,
Contemplates a sunset which is an ashtray,
Chooses to avoid the Casablanca shore,
To serve his time in submarine bars among algae,
Always with a firebird's aspiration for the poetry
            that would stream like mint-leaves from his sleeves.

'If you were as young as me, man,
You could share my togs,
Stick out a foot to tackle mine,

Feint and dodge,
And run your rings around me.'

A Casablanca woman tastes my tears,
Sipping drops of dew wrung from my pained poetry,
      And this makes her all the more thirsty.
She pulls my arm around her waist,
And braids my gathered mint-leaves into an anklet,
She dances, till Casablanca
      dins with the applause of all the night-time drinkers:
A harlot of the night,
A hunger for the night.
And so I danced around a woman –
One who bewitched my verse
      with her hot flesh that would heat no flesh
      so much as it heated mine.
And so we embraced one another,
What delicious footprints on the sand:
Yet didn't they lead to those nets that screw up fish,
To a soul lamenting the out-of-date body, the fleetingness
      of it all,
And to a solo mysticism dreamt up by a mouse?

I sung alone in the port at night,
And ate alone in the port at noon, in its ear-splitting restaurant.
I came back drunk to the Hotel de Paris
And my head was a handful of wind,
I ripped up the poems, and went hunting for the source
  of my dismay:
'Am I the majnoon of a she, conjured up from the depths
  of sleep,

Or have I been a dead man since birth,
       and this bitch but a garland of mint-leaves
       woven over my tomb?
If I wreak havoc on the words, and scatter their damaged
   papers
All around the cell of this hotel-room,
Listen to temptation
And sign my contract with Satan,
Won't this enable me to draw the woman to me
Simply by the power of my mind?'
.............?
.............?
Love but the sweat of fatigue on a forehead;
A beckoning bough that presages the slowest of dawns.

20/3/1979

In Earl's Court

A 'Good morning' for the girl in the antiques
As the cat dozed behind the fanlight.
Same old steps, same old feet,
Bitterness of one who reaches in his pocket
       only to discover there's a hole in it.
My feet, their clumsy wanderlust,
And me listing my first friendships, my foolish acts,
       quoting the adage: 'Still waters run deep!'

I sang along – on the steps of St. Paul`s,
Aped the ways of lovers from a multitude of lands,
Effulgent in the eyes of all the tourists:
       'Would Miss J. drink tea with me in Yassin's?'

I messed my shirt with garish spots
       and declared to the one I loved,
'I'll never drink your fill a second time!'
Later I consoled myself – a poster which I stabbed
       Made such a bloody martyr of the woman.
In the mighty cities, I felt myself an orphan.
Ah, initial impulses, companions!

In Earl's Court I chance to bump into one
       with whom I used to drink.
This is suspicious! I think.
Who would stalk my shadow even unto Earl's Court?

One who might feed the flesh of his brothers
       To the savage talons of his homeland,
Send the defected birds
       back into the darkness of their cage?

I haven't got over it yet, that sudden apprehension,
And when I saw him in Earl's Court,
That one with whom I used to drink,
He hurried to avoid me, as if I were the noxious stink.
Who is following who? Which is afraid of the other?

A 'Good evening' for the girl in the antiques
As the rain drizzled down the fanlight.
Same old steps, same old feet,
Bitterness of one who has saved
            a dark wisdom garnered in this cave,
One in retreat from his day,
Tossed into the folds of blue cold.

I no longer ask about my country,
            as it may ask no more about my fate,
Yet I sing whenever I feel like a song,
            'My sleeves are filled with musk,
                    and my plaits are rich with henna.'

London, 1979

The Empty Quarter

I.
I landed, thanks to a pair of wings,
    a flask of wine and pack of cigarettes.
Peculiar state of exiled human, hoping that some girl
    might actually speak Iraqi in Hyde Park –
My verse without its target butt, my arrow
    careless of its aim.
I am a somnambulist
Borne along by passers-by:
    flanneur among their hastening feet…
But through the glass facade of a Camden shop,
    amid its antique bric-a-brac,
I spied an oil lamp stained by soot
    that once was so familiar!
As if through a lens, I
    saw the mud wall of a house
    above that lantern's copper base.
The glow from its funnel seemed to breathe
    a dragon made of light that hovered there
    on the bellied ceiling of the mats.
At some earlier time I teased out stuff
    into a cloud of coloured fluff
    and threw it in the faces that I came across –
Have been an existentialist; celebrating
    an ambiguous consciousness,
    patching up a mangled dress,
    using the sun's fine yarn.
But at the sight of my lamp in Camden Town
I free myself of the past, that flightless pack
    that weighs my shoulders down.

It is here, and I am here,
Fascinated by a girl, her shoulder bare,
    Flying, flying through the air,
while squirrels fly from branch to branch,
    and she is whispering in my ear:
    'hug me, hug me now!
Hold me, before I disappear.'

Who wouldn't flinch from the cities' blows?
    – cities of the North
    as wet and cold as its forests –
To find solace in stupefaction
    from the dregs of its dark wine
    in the varnished dark of all its bars?
And so I have slept on the sidewalks of my maze,
My verse without its target butt, my arrow
    careless of its aim…
And to support my pain, I lean now on this walking-stick
    That helps my steps towards exile.
A feverish wind weaves a song between my ruins:
    'Our heritage is exile here, not our better times.
    Our heritage is exile here, not our better times.'

2.
But if the dead can give up their tombs
    in the memory of one alive,
If they can abandon all the cities which enclosed them,
If they can cross the dangerous road,
    as we did, barefoot, into the haven of exile,
If they can swathe themselves in the get-up of pirates,
Inhabit silent ships motionlessly afloat
    in the stagnant water of their sea,

Then I can choose the limbo most appropriate for me
In London, under an umbrella,
Celebrating my isolation, free to hang out in the bar –
        Free, that is, from everything but the nude shoulder
Of a girl whispering in my ear,
        'Hug me, hold me now,
        before I disappear.'
She leaves me trapped inside a lamp swinging from a cart
        lurching down a bumpy track.
Is this the way to cross the Empty Quarter?

But the past, the past is like poetry…
        'Poetry, shaven of pate,
        shepherds everything, high on a hill.
A rural man with a flowing gown.'*
He is one who remains forever young, who wants not,
        when I want,
        who runs like grass where I walk,
        and opens like a flower when I just put out my palm.
He lounges on my desk like a book tired by boredom,
        a book with scorched edges.
And when I stare at the restless bells of night,
The past appears like a maid in a jet-black scarf,
        sitting in the presence of the Sultan of Lovers,
        and when her cup runs empty,
        the sword-man fills it up.

3.
Cities are causing overcrowding inside me, and I'm in a
more numerous state than most of Europe's *endroits*. My
alleys know neither discord nor harmony. Neither poet-
ry, nor music, nor painting can fulfil me as much as could
some settlement of my account with history. Autumn is

leaning against the fence of my garden, leaving me a bunch of chestnut leaves which has just fallen from its imagination. I know it's been left for me. Am I not the autumnal man, and doesn't Autumn know it? No difference between the colour of the leaves and the henna on the breasts of the robins. In London, it is pre-Islamic poetry that takes hold of me and make me thirsty. My lips crack, and therefore I anoint them.

4.
I grabbed a girl who said to me
    'You're not much good at flirting.'
I took her to my youthful room.
I was so pissed. And she said:
    'You're not much good,
      even with the most basic words
      in *The Beginners Guide*.'
I told her I was confused,
Making the point
    by stabbing at my forehead with a finger.
I said, 'Why doesn't the Disco
    open in the day?
      If it did the sun could ease my paranoia.'

I feel cold, and orphaned when it's dark,
As if the night subjected me to a body search
In front of the sphinx-like stares of the border police.

5.
'The seer's as blind as I am,
So let us collide in the dark.'*
I said: 'Back home, your steps

went stumbling past,
     until they woke me up.
Oh sheikh, what heavy reason has prompted you to come
     for me?'

'I didn't come for you,' he said.
'You just imagine that I did.
Inheritor, you've taken on the disorder of my soul.
An atom of dust rubs up against its counterpart
In some old verse I wrote down in my book.

Two poets, both accepting
     what their times dictate:
We are two drops,
And this one evaporates
Just as simply as the other freezes.'

6.
'The rust on the knocker is old as night,
And the door is ancient, closed.'****
So down goes my baggage, dumped on the asphalt,
Why would the passers-by
     bother to notice
     a tramp out of time with all tourists?
He stands there, gaunt as a telephone pole,
     hoping, but for what?
No one sees the huge locked door that looms there,
     right in front of him;
A weathered door that stops him
     from breaking into the hubbub of London.
First reaction? Back into the head.
Time is not counted in seconds here, but in the ripples
     as they pass.

I strip off and throw myself in,
And I say to myself, 'Dear self,
      stay very clear of your loss.'
And the answer comes back 'that 'home'
      is a catwalk between abysses,
And he who puts out to sea
Seeking another shore may lose the coast.'[†]
But there is that girl again, ever so near:
'Hug me, hold me, hold me now,
      before I disappear.'

7.
I spoke. 'The wine that got me pissed
      was that enriched by the sun,
But now I am the autumnal one
      (how solemnly intoned).
Heed my boughs, as they divest
      themselves of autumn's leaves
To publish each abandoned nest.
My shadow falls in front of me.
It is a vast abyss.'

She smiled. Her smile brought out a smile.
I said, 'I'm the father of sons.
Their roots are in the present.
Mine prefer the past.
Mine exist to burrow deep,
      delving into what has ceased to be.
All my enigmas are personal now.
They're puzzles only to me.'

Her finger smuggled its secret into my palm.
That very night, her lips were mine;
My head soothed by the pink fan of delight.

8.
There is another inside me.
He gets invited into my Empty Quarter;
Suffers its bleak stretches
    in the middle of the night.
Dune, wind and mirage...
This is my Empty Quarter.

But then there's this tree, my neighbour's,
Laden with its oranges – Sevilles.
Laden, says my memory,
With juice nurtured by the sleep of winter.
How can I harvest these here,
Where all is spoilt by the stench of tar?
Through the window of my silent home I see
Windfalls coated in smoke.
Barbed wire trammels my moments
As insects are caught in a web.

9.
'Slumber now, my weary eyes,
Be as the wings of butterflies
Folded – let the eyelids close.
Oh World, you offer scant repose.
I leave thee now, renounce thee, quit
The trauma of the outcast, flit,
But Oh, to where?'‡

To where? – I let the track repeat,
Closed the book at last,
Drank what was left in the glass,
Gazed at my reflected face
        that offered little peace.
'Millstone of exile, granting no leave
        to return…' ∫
So went the verse, as was its wont.
Christmas, however, had churned out its tidings
Unto a myriad races
        crammed into the morning's market shed.
'Lights out!' I declared in haste
        and fled upstairs, to bed.

20/10/2012

NOTES

* verse from *Plague Lands*.

** verse by Abo Alaa Almaarri.

*** from the poem 'abd al Amir Alhosairi'.

† from 'Paradise of Fools'.

‡ Aria from Bach's cantata BWV82.

∫ From the poem 'Necosia'.

3

Incomprehensible Lesson

The Forgotten City

Late afternoon. The houses shaded.
No, it's pencil strokes of rain.
The birds have flown, their nests abandoned.
The wind applies its whips,
While the tongue freezes amid
Rags and tatters of newsprint.

The birds have flown, their nests abandoned.
And you too, you out-of-place Tuareg,
You've left nothing but footprints.
Come to the waves too late,
    you've stared at them too long.

Echoes of footfalls… leaves in a whirl…
Once a scorcher burnt the wrist of this metropolis.
Now it has cooled to a bracelet of silver
Worn just the once, an age ago, by some forgetful girl.

Wall

I close the door – and the rain lashes my face –
I make for the nearest bar.
Free as any stranger ever is in any city.

I have no kin to get under my skin.
I am a brick in a wall,
Which other walls will soon abut
And then – like that – a fort.
Inside me, muffled by my hat,
I calm the cries of a woman.
The rain must douse her too. The tongue is silenced.

Two glasses, garçon.
Yes, one is for me.
My friend is… on her way.
You'll know her by her woollen coat.

The waiter, familiar with the type,
Plumbs the obsessive mindset to its heart.
Another will not tolerate delay,
He nods therefore – then scoots away.

The Scavengers

These scavengers for wood beside the Thames:
I take in their glutinous, tar-like stink.
In the sieve of their thick, matted hair,
They trap all the dirt and the darkness of London.
Their exile nourishes their silence.

I too am a scavenger,
I too am an exile,
Shouldn't I join them,
Born again,
A scavenger for words beside the Thames?

Their exile seems a good deal worse than mine.
I see their make-shift shelters from the rain –
Boxes, slumped against concrete –
In which they huddle, the deadbeat,
Alcoholic spirits,
Weighted down by numbness.

For warmth, I wait in a phone booth, staring out.
A frozen sparrow lands nearby. A woman
Breathes a promise on a pane. My palm
Throbs between my cheek and what it is I rest against.

That odour plugs my nostrils like a comforter.
I sense the alluvial sludge of each year's residue.
A train on some nearby platform sighs.
The suitcase cannot move.

Seeing and Pleading

My father, now in white, undergoes his agonies,
And the god I have always denied enters the house.
My mother, sisters, brother, in a half-circle there,
Haven't noticed, haven't raised their eyes.
I am the only one to have seen him coming in.
And I'm the only one who is trying not to look at him.

The god is crying, this god I have always denied,
For isn't he full of his always infinite pity?
The shadow of death hangs over the family.
Soon there'll be nothing but darkness.
An emptiness will engulf my father's body.

There is a listening though.
Our sole right is to plead.
We cannot ask the question which is always on our lips,
Aching to be spoken.
From frustration such as this bitterness must flow.

But here is the god, hunched over, blasted by time,
A ruined place, sole refuge now
For refugees from who knows where.
He slips away, so quietly,
But, doggedly, unseen, I follow after,

Both of us lost, in the way some stars get lost,
Through desert dust, and mirages
Of water which recede from us forever
Like travellers who went before…
Their bones repeat the moaning of the wind
Across these wind-lashed spaces, the wolves not far behind.

There is a listening though.
Our sole right is to plead.
We cannot ask the question which is always on our lips,
Aching to be spoken.
From frustration such as ours bitterness must flow.

The Painting

Gloom steeps the memory.
Light though filters through
Onto a wooden table top: a joint of beef,
A match perhaps, some scattered cigarettes,
A glass or two.

It's dinner time for me and you.
Our foreheads bend towards each other,
Yellowing like ivory.
Caught in that shaft of light,
We weave together threads of the silence between us,
Taking up such as may snag in its web,
And making sure we never ever touch.

The Goal-Keeper

Louis! Ah,
What a Wonderful World,
Your voice, rough as the bark of a tree,
Threads through this lobby like hope.

Phosphorescent at your words,
I glow above this book I thumb,
Beside the stove that keeps me warm.

How strange life's been to me –
One minute full, the next mere dregs,
Eyes a-brim with tears – or glee.

I am a goalkeeper.
Strikers with no ball make me wary,
Seeing a void blue infinity
Between some clatter of legs.

Black Ink

The darkness of this night is greater
Than the power of a sultan.
Ink from my books, shelf upon shelf of them,
Pours down the curtains.
Every book is an overturned inkwell.

Patience, I say. Day will dawn,
And the colours will spill everywhere.
Snatching up the brush,
I try to paint the walls green,
The curtains rosy pink,
But now the waves come washing in:
Blue – with light's sporadic wink.

The Tale

There was a bunch of violets I let fall
Into the depths of a well.
The sun still gleamed on them, but they soon
Lost their colour, then they lost their smell.

And so I played with time, not realising
That the violets would not be amused.
And today, I know this story has to do with my boyhood
And days which speak to me sadly, knowingly too.

Each petal seems like some word that's especially tender,
And what was I doing? Just having fun with its innocence,
Letting it fall, letting it fall into a well of meaning
Only to grow confused.

The word becomes like an instrument
Probing a wound on the mend simply to breach it again.
And then I see in the well a widow's tears.
How is it all this appears – out of a word?

With its garden in sight, I can't help but become
A coat beaten back by the rain.
It's the shadow of the unseen in the arbour,
Isolation's patron, always stooping over what I write.

The Night Drives Its Nails

Winter strips the tree to one solitary nest.
Rain drips through its mesh of twigs.
And then the snow embalms it in a cotton shroud.

That nest is as heavy now
As the silence gluing up my ears
Or the smoke weighing down my lungs.
It penetrates my dreams, where night is driving on –
Driving on and driving in its nails.

Winter of God

In the summer, Lord, we laze,
Dreaming through our birthright.
Spring and autumn, at your behest,
Get reserved for planting and for harvest
With respect to winter, your especial favourite.

Summer we recall
For the friend who comes out of his shell,
For the neighbour's daughter
Who scampers nude beneath the tossing palm,
For the angel with a mother's name,
And for a father who has lasted well.

All pretty futile, compared to your winter!
That is when you teach us… to revise.
The day of celebration is for sure our day of doom.
For even as we seize
The chance to reap experience,
You hasten to desert us:
As if the proffered fruit had failed to please.

Our dreams grow so green beneath your magnifying sky.
And the stars gleam – oh so rosily –
Nipples of your virgins in the hour of their fertility.

Lord, once again, we take shelter in prayer,
Asking for a respite from memory,
Asking for the autumn depths to store up our desire,
And for the spring to offer its dark promise of fertility.

Yet nothing can be deeper than your winter and its treachery.

The Muse

An empty glass of wine in the palm of my right hand,
While the scented corner of the veil
Worn by my inspiration
Gets rubbed between thumb and finger.

The foothills killed off by winter will again be covered in grass;
And the streams will begin to burble to each other.
The crickets will keep the birds awake,
And I will lay my cushion down
By the bank of the Tigris
Once more, as before, just before sunset.

The glass will get replenished with some red
Into which the evening's dark will seep;
The silver of the moon will coat its face

And the waist of the one who returns
At last to my cushion
Will rest against my other palm,
Her fine robe utterly undone.

For the Thousandth Time

1.

For the thousandth time, I'm in transit,
I dump my suitcase down in some modest room,
Open for the thousandth time a window,
And there I am across the street, lugging along my suitcase.

2.

Now I feel listless. I am at the airport.
The flight has been called, and I enter the bottleneck,
Hemmed in by strange languages.

3.

And when poetry assails me I'm extinguished,
Grandiloquent day is unable to counter its night,
Meanings tar the reader too.
This fruit is bad for the birds.

4.

Of course I love the clouds that sail by ever more swiftly,
The wind that bends the palms,
And the fire of the sunset that glows above the chimneys,
But then there are barbs to my queries:
Why put faith in any of these images?

5.

Say the need for a nap descends on me,
And the dreamy bird of desire rises from its nest,
What am I but a blind man somewhere
Wrapped in his coat as if inside a womb?
I can cope like this, I really can.
But the bird in my dream retreats to its nest at dawn.

6.
I see my country starving,
All the pollen floating away in the wind.
There, the palm trees might as well be gravestones
For those who cling on,
While those who migrate.
Are skeletons swinging on the line.

7.
Did I say goodbye and turn away, or was it the country
That turned and left me to starve?

8.
My fear is of keeping going, crawling along
      the tunnel with the rest.
There has to be light at the end, yes, but what does it show?
The bullets, the bullets I've faced,
The bullets they've faced, who continue crawling along it.

9.
I will write about our brothers:
How they've been snatched up by talons,
Taken by a hawk. I'll write about the silence –
That adhesive smeared across the lips –

About the words that weave webs
And the words that are words no more.
And I will write about wisdom repeating itself
As often as the sand in an hour-glass;

About the corpses that vanish into the bowels of our past.

10.

And I have a date up ahead, with the backstreets
    of my childhood;
With the low houses, the windows, the telegraph poles,
    the palm trees,
The scattered mud and the tar
    filming the stagnant water there;
All of it wrapped in moonlight's foil.
    And the sand throws one soft veil
Around me, as if I were naked,
    although there is no sound,
No sound to the wind. The thorny tumbleweed
    rolls on its way up ahead.
There's no one here but me. But here, here is nowhere.
There's just the pulse of an alarm whose time
    has not yet come.

11.

Tigris, are you listening,
    as I am, to the singers on the bridge?
They leave one side of the city for the other!
They are getting from there to here, and their songs
Get from their lungs into mine,
    along with their tobacco smoke.
Do you hear the sound coming from that well?
Yes, it's the muezzein.
Oh, I remember this well.
It was a minaret once upon a time,
But then turned upside down.

12.

Every building here, opera house, museum,
Underground tunnel, even my home
Conspires to remind me how far away I am.
Following a thread through the maze

No longer gets me anywhere.
Only you, my woman made of jasmine and desire
Have the power to slow the rush of time
And stop the infernal humming from the wire.

The Crack

She appeared to me naked,
                   kohl on her eyes,
Lips made red by a pomegranate's peel,
Palm pollen powdered on her cheeks,
An apricot for each of her nipples.

Barefoot, she was, with opened palms,
                   as if for her fortune to be read…
Dumbstruck, was I, who had never dwelt in my reflection.
Yes, but now this dumbness obliged me to reside
                   there in the hall of all her mirrors.

She irrigated passion seductively with wine,
And so I kept pace as she staggered off the pavement.
And as I feared she would, she smashed me like a pitcher.
Though I tried to piece myself together,
I saw in this shattering an amulet for exile.
                   I could hide myself in this.
This is what love is! So I fooled myself,
So I gave up history for myth.

As for my love, she became
                   fragments of a mirror, nothing more.
I stared into these, and at my shattered visage,
Trying to grasp the whole from the splinter.

What can you tell from a crack?

In the Dark We Listen

Two bodies in the dark
Listen to Ravel's *Bolero.*
Fingers drum
On each other
That repeating rhythm,
Hoping to succumb
To one another.

By the dim glimmer of a pane,
I may make out the shadow of a smile,
A smile that I return,
Sensing the pulse of desire
Through that parted robe.
I am what seems wanted,
but as if unseeing,
I pursue my stumbling stick instead.

I just chucked my words
Into a well with no echo,
Let my fingers rest
From chasing the rhythm.
Here an arm flung out, from me
Towards that hint of a body.

Lover hugging lover,
Bottomless as wells
Too deep to quench each other.

Dialogue with Waves

'You were just a pebble, and now you've gathered moss!'
The wave says to me, as I lie on the beach.
Then in my turn I say to the pebble next to me:
'Hey there, have you gathered moss?'

And it answers 'Yes, I've gathered moss,
But time's lumbering turtle,
Rummages still through all my souvenirs.'
'Rummages through the sea,' I say,

'Since out-of-date time survives there.'
Today, as I enter my thousandth year,
I consider how each is a friend of the waves.
Their deep blue iris watches over us,

Coating one and all with velvet moss,
Observing, sending us messages,
Snails, shells and squid keep us company.
Fish are taught to cleanse the pores.

We are the sea's green pebbles, and our eyes
Never lose sight of the sand of history
Rising in its storms over dunes and skulls.
How curious it feels!

Washed up on the shore, the rain
Laving our foreheads, the wind blindly
Fumbling us. Our lively debate with the waves
Remaining a constant within us!

The Patrolman

You are dogging my steps! You, Patrolman,
Entrusted with the dreams of sleepers.
The plod of your step nudges an echo
Out of the dirt of the night, and darkness
Wobbles like a wagon's lantern on a uneven road.
How much longer must my body take
The lurching of this journey I'm embarked upon?

I feel your possession of me – even in my clothes.
What flutters between my legs is fear,
Fear like the wings of a dove
Eager to fly but incapable of flight.

I feel you in the refuse and rubbish of my years.
And you've spread to my lungs, so that I cough
And you hear me cough! I sense your presence too
At the stealthy moment of my break-out.

Your eyes, your eyes are like holes in a sack,
With the goods simply trickling away.
All my own barbed barriers
Vibrate to the blasts of your whistle,
Fracturing the night's metallic shell.
Even the wintry moon
Grinds her teeth in panic-stricken jaws!

Our guardian, keeper of the dark…

Incomprehensible Lesson

At the hour of sunset, autumn clouds
    are scattered sheep drifting towards the distance.
The six stalks of our feet dangle over the lip
    of the clay oven.
We hang around like that, eat warm bread,
    while counting the sheep of the days we have left:
Happy days that remain before we're packed off to school.

My mother comes to shepherd us from time to time.
I listen to the birds,
    and to what they want me to report to her
    as they pass in their migratory convoys.
The message is for anybody waiting,
    waiting like her, while the birds are here
    for a little while, and then they're off on their way again.
It is as if this is teaching me some incomprehensible lesson.
Already I'm a poet in my prime.

It is thus that a hidden sigh
    lifts me above my brothers,
Higher than the palm tree,
And then I'm back, cold from the heights,
Back within their captivating warm.

All too soon, the sharp-clawed hawk will snatch me,
The hawk that hovers over my life,
A life, which in its vigilance
    resembles a city under siege.
And only in the negligence of time
    can the hawk stoop, drop onto me
The present moment, heavy as a millstone.

And here I am, ground round and round as it turns,
    grinding no flour whatsoever.
I can't help counting the days that are left
And what the days have in store
Before I have to revise that incomprehensible lesson.

The Balloon

A cloud on the horizon extends its moistened tongue
    like a dog licking my forehead.
I rise with a blaze glowing here inside me,
Bright as ever was my first delight.

 My face reflects the sun.
The swirling air supports me, I answer to its whim.
And even if the compass is a quandary
Or the air burns my lungs, or the fire beneath me dies,
I will continue as this empty circle
Heat alone encourages to rise,
    until I burst like Icarus into flame.

The Flame

I cannot look away.
Whispering in a corner,
Removed from passers-by.
I see a woman in shock:

'You didn't get to me, when the heater
   set fire to our home.
You weren't nearly as whole as the man you seemed.
You looked shorter than you were
   because you were crushed by fear.
Your blood had dried up within you.
You saw me quite close up, when the fabric caught alight,
And you turned the page on that vision
   as if it were only a thing in a book.
But I am what you will read, wherever your eyes may look:
On the earth seen from the window of a plane,
On memory's page, tale of indelible scars,
On the wall which is the legacy of previous city walls.

You will never be able to put it down, this book
You'll continue to hover before
Until you reach that decisive moment
In your own rotation towards fire.

I see a woman in shock,
Removed from passers-by,
Whispering in a corner.
I cannot look away.

No One Comes to Join Me

No one comes to join me in this tavern
Situated somewhere
   so desolate.
A wooden chair, well worn,
With a view of the deep,
Contemplates a sea-gulled horizon…
A blind man supporting some timid little cripple…

The fisherman leaves his nets,
Only to be trammeled in the mesh of marsh fever.
The sea claws him back, drags him by the scruff
Back to where a pirate is waiting.

I have travelled by train through a dream,
Tunnel after tunnel,
Shows me through its windows
   the irritable nerve inside its ebony –
As many scenes as seconds to the journey:

Light reveals these many-coloured masks:
The hedgehog with barbed-wire for spines.
The books on the shelves
   bleeding from their wounds,
And here is a mouth with claws.

It was as if I had seen you undress,
   seen you hang your clothes
On the back of that wooden chair, well worn,
With a view of the deep
   and its sea-gulled horizon.

I was that boyhood, that boyish voyeur
Watching from the tavern...

How long will it take the poet
    to gain for himself the confidence of pain?
And will the lover inside him,
    with his wrinkled mouth-wisdom,
Ever earn the right to call your name?

I may not cheat the worn-out robes,
Dare not disappear on wings
    that would carry me away from you.
When you emerge
    from the tunnel of my skeptical surmise,
I will say to you:

You know I kid myself that some fine day,
    which is not to be attributed to London,
I'll come across the shadow of a girl writing poetry,
A poetry that trips on the shadow of its pain,
    and nearly lose my own footing.
Love's a fine thing, yet it fills me with shame.

Usual Story

And my friend
Was immersed in Sufi texts
And he liked to maintain that the world
Meant less to him than a goat's fart.

And my friend was intrigued by the bar
   and his bar-room mates,
Weren't they the key to some expansive vision?

But the world sharpens more than one sword:
The Other is a sword,
   and the Word is a sword,
And the Homeland held a sword above each head,
And the Leader held up the swordsmen.

And so my friend withdrew
   into aloneness.
Didn't trust anyone but his own shadow,
And one day, which was filled with Iraqi night,
His shadow wife hid a wire beneath the bed,
Took off all her clothes, and flirtatiously
Begged him to vilify the state.

And my friend
Is now a prisoner
Wrapped in the national flag,
Learning how to love the Leader's photo.

The Absent

Our grandchildren, then. It's up to them.
They will inherit our features. And they will tell
Our stories, share each exploit,
Fertilise thus our rank remains perhaps.
We each may earn a tombstone, and poets get a call
To etch what we inspired on it. Or perhaps
The mirrors that have recorded what we did
Will simply be interred. The Kalifa brigade
Will see to it the site has no visitors.
The body of our work will be flayed,
Or enslaved to some justified ruler perhaps.

Will we engender pilots in the seas of night
Or muggers in urban jungles?
Perhaps we'll leave no trace at all
Beyond that of a rat
Glued inside the damp trap of nothingness.

To the Reader

You will read my poetry
And it will be your dwelling for a while,
The air infused by the burning of a matchstick,
And you will wince, confused.
From what rupture is this smoke coming from?
From what hot repository of torment?

You will read my poetry,
And sense that the words may fly like birds
Beautiful and healthy,
Yet when they fly they leave their meanings
On the lines, so they excrete their dark,
And they are exposed forever in their flight.

Whereas with closure, you can escape the book.

The Isle of the Dead

After Arnold Böcklin and Rachmaninoff

Just as the flywheel of time grows rusty in the clock,
Or the scream freezes on the face of the fearful
   fixed in a photo on some page,
So the water calms around that isle.

A blessed isle of silence and sad light,
Where clumps of dismal cypress hug each other.
Gulls may encircle it, fruit may frame it, however
It remains a cage which is a citadel.
There is a boatman and there is a boat,
And there is the spectre, upright though afloat,
Approaching there that rocky island mass.

And as the indifferent sun descends,
The new arrival steps down
   carefully onto the rocks.
And the boatman quietly turns his boat
Back towards the shore of life
Where another figure waits to cross.

Over Hastily

Over hastily he picks up his bag
   in a field of flowers.
In a rush, he gets out
    a ticket for a train.

Confused in his seat, he waits
For the train to stop at a minefield.
    The war has only just started.
He drops down into its new-dug trench,
Among the slaughtered soldiers.

He takes a mine as a pillow and he sleeps.